GREAT MARQUES POSTER BOOK

MERCEDES-BENZ

CHRIS HARVEY

OCTOPUS BOOKS

Contents

First published in 1986 by Octopus Books Limited, 59 Grosvenor Street, London W1

© 1986 Octopus Books Limited

ISBN 0 7064 2501 4

Produced by Mandarin Publishers Limited, 22a Westlands Road, Quarry Bay, Hong Kong

Printed in Hong Kong

Acknowledgements
All cars were provided by the Daimler-Benz Museum, Germany, with the following exceptions: Coys of Kensington (page 17), Richard Grey (25), R. D. Lloyd (39), David Prior (41), Mercedes-Benz (UK) Ltd (43, 45), The Patrick Collection (47)

The Publishers would like to thank Daimler-Benz AG of Stuttgart for permission to reproduce their registered trademark.

Special photography: Rainer Schlegelmilch, Andrew Morland (pages 17, 25, 39, 41), Laurie J. Caddell (1, 43, 45), Ian Dawson (47)

Page 1 The famous three-pointed star of Mercedes-Benz
Page 3 1936 Mercedes-Benz 540K

Introduction

Daimler-Benz, which makes Mercedes cars, is not only recognized as the oldest surviving car maker in the world, but one that is still ahead of almost every other when it comes to technological perfection. The company's craftsmanship is as unquestioned as the integrity of its design.

The story of Mercedes started with Karl Benz, who in 1885 produced the world's first motorized carriage for use on the road – a tricycle – with four-wheeled cars to follow. His wife, Birta, was one of the earliest serious motorists when she took their children on a five-day proving trip from the family headquarters in Mannheim to Pforzheim and back in 1888.

During that time, another great engineer, Gottlieb Daimler, was founding the company that would prove to be Benz's greatest rival, at Bad Cannstatt, only some 96 km (60 miles) away. Daimler and Benz never met, but their early products were among the most advanced in a fledgling motor industry. Inevitably, they attracted passionate admirers, none more so than the Austrian Emil Jellinek who, when he became a Daimler director, named the cars he sold after his lovely young daughter, Mercédès.

The first Mercédès set new standards in design and engineering when it was introduced in 1901. Within a few years all German Daimlers were called Mercedes (the accents were soon dropped), though allied firms continued to make cars under the Daimler name in Britain and Austria. Benz was stubborn at first and refused to modernize his designs to compete with the new Mercedes menace, now based at Stuttgart. His sales plunged. He then came back with such a vengeance that the rival marques from Mannheim and Stuttgart struggled for supremacy throughout the years leading up to World War 1. The Blitzen Benz of 1909 became one of the world's most successful racing cars and held the land speed record at 228 km/h (141.7 mph) for a number of years. Mercedes, not to be outdone, produced superb grand prix cars, including the fantastic overhead-camshaft machine of 1914 that was to revolutionize engine design. By then, the Daimler and Benz companies had become industrial giants in the manufacture not only of cars, but also of commercial vehicles and aero engines. The war nearly killed them, however, as Germany wrestled with runaway inflation

in its aftermath. Finally they agreed to cut costs by rationalizing their ranges and research and then, three years later, in 1926, to a complete merger as Daimler-Benz, with Mercedes-Benz as the marque name. The legend of the three-pointed star began in earnest, as the Daimler star was welded into a circle derived from the Benz laurel wreath emblem.

Early chief engineers included Paul Daimler, son of Gottlieb, and the legendary Dr Ferdinand Porsche, who had made his name with the Austrian subsidiary of the Daimler empire. The Benz designs continued to provide workaday basic models, while the Mercedes tradition was never more evident than in some of the glamorous cars made in the late 1920s and early 1930s, such as the fabulous supercharged SSK. It was machines like this, in the hands of drivers such as Rudolf Caracciola, that took Mercedes-Benz back to the top in competition, and this sporting image was reinforced by its quite incredibly powerful grand prix cars. Their speeds approached 320 km/h (200 mph) in a five-year battle with the rival German concern, Auto Union, that was to leave the world gasping on the eve of World War 2. The ordinary road cars felt the benefit, with all-independent suspension as early as 1931.

World War 2 all but finished Daimler-Benz: its factories were bombed into ruins. With incredible tenacity the firm fought back to carry on where it had left off, marketing thoroughly dependable basic cars while perfecting a prodigious brood of racers that showed themselves to be the best in the world in the 1950s. This competition success was achieved at great expense – not only in monetary terms, but in engineering time – and after its mark had been made Daimler-Benz withdrew to concentrate on providing front-running road cars.

Fuel injection developed by Mercedes-Benz from the racing machines and diesel economy cars put the company in the vanguard of technical development. However, this was a stubborn firm and it clung to problematic swing-axle suspension for decades before finally abandoning it for more conventional springing on its thoroughly modern cars of today: all magnificently engineered machines that have a reputation second to none for durability and dependable design.

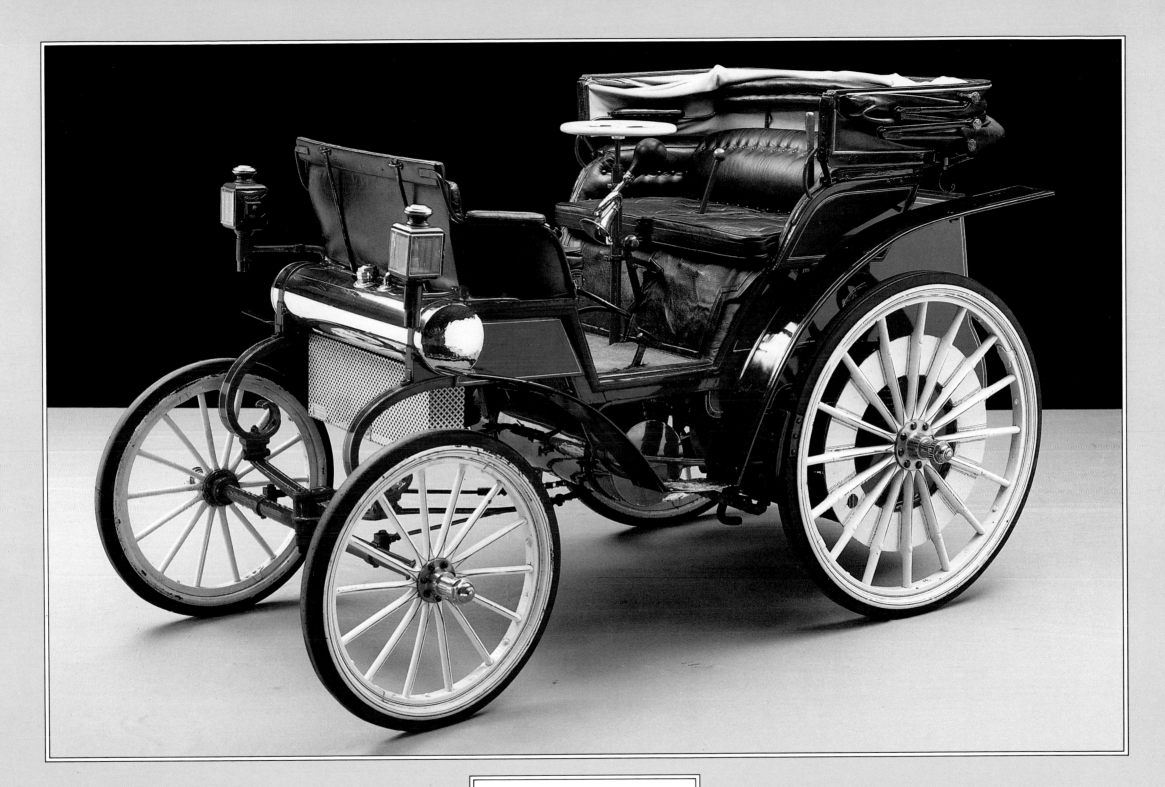

1894 Benz Vis-à-Vis

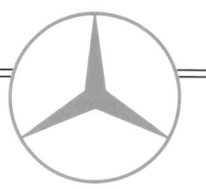

Benz Vis-à-Vis

Karl Benz had to start from scratch when designing his first vehicles, with no real precedent to guide him. When viewed in this context, his designs seem remarkably well conceived. His first engine produced just under 1 brake horsepower, although this output had been increased to 4 by the time production of his 1894 Vis-à-Vis got under way. In the early vehicles, the cumbersome single-cylinder engine was mounted on a flimsy chassis with a huge horizontal flywheel intended to prevent the turbulent power unit sending the chassis spinning. As it happened, this type of flywheel was not necessary, but the conservative Benz did not abandon it until 1897, after the Vis-à-Vis car had become well established. In the same way, he retained his other early ideas, many of which can still be seen in today's cars. His engine was cooled by water and fired by electric ignition, with mechanically operated inlet valves. These cars also had a very clever differential to allow the large cart-style rear wheels to rotate at different speeds on corners – although it took Benz several years to solve the enigma of steering the front wheels.

His 1894 Vis-à-Vis, so called because it accommodated its passengers in face-to-face seating, had a simple cart-type front axle, swung from left to right and back again by chains operated from one of the world's first steering wheels, at a time when most of his rivals used a boat-style tiller. Doubtless, Benz's steering wheel was developed from railway practice, as were his foot-operated brakes with shoes bearing directly on the rubber linings of the solid rear wheels. The handling has to be imagined, with its twitchy steering on a springy chassis powered by a thudding engine turning over at about 500 rpm, followed by hasty disengagement of mighty cogs and the rasping of cast-iron brake shoes as the whole contraption was brought to a halt.

Clever marketing, however, overcame early opposition, and by 1894 there were four Benz models in production: the Victoria, with just two seats, at RM3950; the three-seater Vis-à-Vis at RM4150; the Phaeton with four seats arranged face to face behind a conductor, with the occupants covered by a shade and curtains, at RM4800; and the massive six-seater Landauer, which bore a strikingly close resemblance to a state carriage and was priced at RM6000.

ENGINE		CHASSIS	
Type	Water-cooled	Frame	Tubular construction
No. of cylinders	1	Wheelbase mm	1650
Bore/stroke mm	130 × 150	Track – front mm	1300
Displacement cc	1990	Track – rear mm	1300
Valve operation	2, mechanical linkage	Suspension – front	Half-elliptic springs, beam axle
Sparkplugs per cyl.	1		
Compression ratio	2:1	Suspension – rear	Half-elliptic springs, live axle
Induction	Gravity feed		
BHP	4	Brakes	2 shoes on rear rims
Transmission	Two-speed manual gearbox		
		PERFORMANCE	
		Maximum speed	30 km/h)18.6 mph)
		Fuel consumption	25 litres/100 km (11.3 mpg)

1909 Benz 20/35

Benz 20/35

Once Karl Benz had established his own principles about how a car should be constructed, it took many years to persuade him that there were other ways of doing it. He stuck to his old-fashioned engineering until 1904, and then plunging sales in the face of competition, such as that of Daimler's more advanced machinery, caused Benz to alter his ideas. He then brought himself vigorously up to date, introducing new four-cylinder models to replace the twins which had taken over from earlier single-cylinder efforts.

This renaissance resulted in a number of racing successes; the Benz competition vehicles became direct rivals of the massive Mercedes models produced by Daimler. Road cars benefited as a result with a new range introduced by Benz in 1908 as the 10/18, 10/20 and 20/35: the first figures in these coded names indicate the horsepower that was taxable in Germany at the time, and the second figures the actual output of their four-cylinder engines. All three models had a monobloc L-head side-valve power unit, with shaft drive via a torque tube to a live rear axle, which still featured Benz's famous differential. Until that time, engineers had been doubtful whether shaft drive could reliably convey the power generated by their large and efficient engines, and tended to stick to tried and trusted chains. Naturally, these exposed chain drives suffered badly from mud and dust on the road and had to be cleaned and oiled every day. This became a primary reason for employing a chauffeur: if you could afford to buy a large, powerful car which – of necessity – had chain drive, you could afford to pay somebody to maintain it as a full-time job. Vehicles such as the Benz 20/35, incorporating shaft drive, represented a considerable advance because they did not need this degree of maintenance, although the cost was still high enough to limit them firmly to the chauffeur-employing classes.

Such cars had progressed to four-speed transmission by 1909, with an altogether more modern body inspired by competitors like Mercedes; they continued, essentially unchanged, until around 1920. Labour was still cheap in those days and the amount of skilled work that went into their construction has made them enduring classics – even the roof rack represents a work of art.

ENGINE		CHASSIS	
Type	In-line, water-cooled	Frame	Channel section
No. of cylinders	4	Wheelbase mm	3210
Bore/stroke mm	105 × 150	Track – front mm	1440
Displacement cc	5195	Track – rear mm	1440
Valve operation	2 per cylinder, pushrod	Suspension – front	Half-elliptic springs, beam axle
Sparkplugs per cyl.	1	Suspension – rear	Half-elliptic springs, live axle
Compression ratio	3:1		
Induction	Benz *Spritzdüsenvergaser* carburettor	Brakes	Two water-cooled drums on chain-drive countershaft
BHP	35	**PERFORMANCE**	
Transmission	Four-speed manual gearbox	Maximum speed	75 km/h (46.6 mph)
		Fuel consumption	22 litres/100 km (12.8 mpg)

1910 Mercedes 16/40

Mercedes 16/40

The name Mercedes sprang to prominence with a series of inspiring big cars during the early part of the 20th century. All were derived from chief designer Wilhelm Maybach's brilliant 1901 concept, and were produced in both competition and touring versions. A bewildering number of models was made. This meant that their prices were very high because production had to start from scratch for each car. The Daimler company was also beset by personality clashes immediately after Gottlieb Daimler's death which resulted in his long-time collaborator, Maybach, leaving in 1907 to produce his own still more gargantuan cars and aero engines. Emil Jellinek, who had given the name Mercedes to Daimler, also left at the same time, but Gottlieb Daimler's son Paul – who had been running the company's Austrian subsidiary – returned to reorganize the engineering side.

He improved the existing models and, more importantly, he introduced a new smaller and cheaper generation of cars bearing the Mercedes name to sell alongside the mammoths. Other obvious technical changes included a switch throughout from chain to shaft drive, and the use of the live rear axle, which continued to be a mainstay of car production until recently. The Maybach cars, which stayed in production, ranged from 70 hp up to 120 hp, whereas Paul Daimler's first models were the 8/18, 10/20, 14/30, 22/40 and 28/60. These quickly became popular and Daimler's business expanded mightily as a result, although the Maybach cars continued to be the flagships.

Ever anxious to be seen to be in the vanguard of technical development, Daimler fell in with a fashion then sweeping Europe by obtaining a licence to build and use the sleeve-valve engine designed by the American Knight company. It was thought that these engines would be more attractive because they were quieter than those using poppet valves, and they were accordingly introduced on Daimler's new Mercedes 10/30, 16/40 and 16/45 cars in 1910. Lubrication proved to be a problem, however, with the engines using a lot of oil, and they continued in production for only a few years.

It was also fashionable at that time to update your car by fitting new bodywork every few years; this surviving example of a 1910 16/40 looks quite normal with the coachwork used in 1913.

ENGINE		CHASSIS	
Type	In-line, water-cooled	**Frame**	Channel section
No. of cylinders	4	**Wheelbase mm**	2960
Bore/stroke mm	100 × 130	**Track – front mm**	1300
Displacement cc	4080	**Track – rear mm**	1300
Valve operation	Knight sleeve	**Suspension – front**	Half-elliptic springs, beam axle
Sparkplugs per cyl.	1		
Compression ratio	4 : 1	**Suspension – rear**	Half-elliptic springs, live axle
Induction	*Kolbenvergaser* carburettor		
		Brakes	Drums, rear only
BHP	40		
Transmission	Four-speed manual gearbox	**PERFORMANCE**	
		Maximum speed	80 km/h (49.7 mph)
		Fuel consumption	23 litres/100 km (12.28 mpg)

1912 Benz 8/20

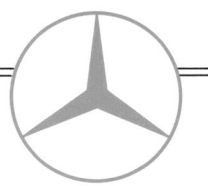

Benz 8/20

The smallest Benz produced immediately before World War 1 was the 8/20, which was simply a slightly updated version of the 10/20, but a formidable car nonetheless. The world's oldest motoring magazine, *The Autocar*, then a veteran of 16 years, described the 'Baby Benz' as a full-sized touring car in miniature. It noted that its hood could be raised and lowered by one man, on his own, and that its engine was so quiet that the occupants could hear remarks made by people on the footpaths alongside the road while it was ticking over in a traffic jam: tappet clatter and carburettor hiss were seemingly non-existent. *The Autocar* considered the engine to be excellently balanced with a distinct vibration period only occurring at around 50 km/h (32 mph). It was best to avoid this speed, all others being smooth and quiet.

The suspension also met the demands of the day with ease, severe potholes between Shepherd's Bush and Acton, in West London, being 'barely noticeable'. In fact, *The Autocar* noted: 'Riding in the Benz caused us to cease to wonder why certain German competitors in the Prince Henry Tour made such splendid averages.' Obviously, the Baby Benz had benefited considerably from the competition exploits of the bigger cars. Its steering was considered particularly good and 'quite irreversible'.

Having survived the perils of Acton, *The Autocar's* test team headed for Uxbridge via Ealing, and then followed the main Oxford road to Beaconsfield with the intention of doing 'some lane work among the Chiltern Hills'. The Baby Benz revelled in such conditions despite carrying a full load of four passengers. It climbed the notorious Rectory Hill at Amersham (with its gradient of 1 in 7 'or worse') in first gear, and took half the nearby Gore Hill in third gear before having to resort to second and, ultimately, first again at the top. What might have happened had it failed to surmount either gradient is not clear, although shedding some of its load seems a probable solution.

The Benz was well equipped, with two speedometers. One was an A.T., driven from the gearbox, and the other, a Star, from one front wheel. They agreed, fortunately, in their evaluation of the car's speed. The magnificent serpentine horn, curling along the side of the car, failed to arouse comment. Presumably it was considered a common fitting at the time.

ENGINE		CHASSIS	
Type	In-line water-cooled	**Frame**	Channel section
No. of cylinders	4	**Wheelbase mm**	2850
Bore/stroke mm	72 × 120	**Track – front mm**	1350
Displacement cc	1950	**Track – rear mm**	1350
Valve operation	2 per cylinder, pushrod	**Suspension – front**	Half-elliptic springs, beam axle
Sparkplugs per cyl.	1	**Suspension – rear**	Half-elliptic springs, live axle
Compression ratio	4.5 : 1		
Induction	Zenith carburettor	**Brakes**	Drums, rear only
BHP	20		
Transmission	Four-speed manual gearbox	PERFORMANCE	
		Maximum speed	62 km/h (38.5 mph)
		Fuel consumption	15 litres/100 km (18.8 mpg)

1924 Mercedes 24/100/140

Mercedes 24/100/140

The first supercharged Mercedes sports cars were Paul Daimler's last great work before he retired in 1922 – to be succeeded by the legendary Dr Ferdinand Porsche, who had worked with him at Daimler's Austrian subsidiary even before it became the independent Austro-Daimler concern.

Porsche's first work for the parent company was to improve the supercharged cars: the last such to bear the name Mercedes alone, rather than Mercedes-Benz. They were logical evolutions from the 6/25/40 and 10/40/65, using technology developed on a 2-litre supercharged eight-cylinder racer which was designed by Dr Porsche in 1923.

The specifications of the 3920 cc 15/70/100 and the 6240 cc 24/100/140 were typical of the biggest and most expensive sporting cars built in the 1920s. They had a long-wheelbase, channel-section, pressed-steel chassis, with an I-section front axle, live beam rear axle and very stiff springs and friction-type shock absorbers. Their roadholding depended almost entirely on their great weight and flexing chassis, with the ride made tolerable only by the length of the wheelbase and the depth of the upholstery.

The two cars' six-cylinder engines were basically the same as each other, except in size, and kept the method of supercharger operation established by the earlier cars in 1921. The three years between the introduction of the earlier models and that of the new cars late in 1924 had been used to perfect the supercharger's method of induction, so that it now became a 'blower' pushing pressurized air into the carburettor before the fuel was added, rather than driving the fuel/air mixture from the carburettor into the engine. The new power units were of more advanced design, featuring an overhead camshaft to operate the valves: a more efficient system pioneered on a Mercedes grand prix car that had been built in 1914.

The mechanically operated brakes on all four wheels were also a relatively new feature, even though they did not work very well. Despite the inadequacies of the brakes and the top-heavy handling, partly caused by massive bodywork, these great V-radiatored cars became the kings of the open road in Europe, at a starting price of RM24,000. By 1924, however, Germany was being consumed by rampant inflation and they became the last cars to be designed by the independent Daimler concern before its merger with Benz.

ENGINE		CHASSIS	
Type	In-line, water-cooled	Frame	Channel section, cross-braced
No. of cylinders	6		
Bore/stroke mm	94 × 150	Wheelbase mm	3750
Displacement cc	6240	Track – front mm	1430
Valve operation	2 per cylinder, overhead camshaft	Track – rear mm	1430
		Suspension – front	Half-elliptic springs, beam axle
Sparkplugs per cyl.	1		
Compression ratio	5:1	Suspension – rear	Half-elliptic springs, live axle
Induction	Mercedes carburettor, Roots supercharger	Brakes	Drums front and rear
		PERFORMANCE	
BHP	140	Maximum speed	115 km/h (71.5 mph)
Transmission	Four-speed manual gearbox	Fuel consumption	25 litres/100 km (11.3 mpg)

1924 Mercedes 10/40/65

Mercedes 10/40/65

Total defeat in World War 1 left Germany's economy in ruins, and even industrial giants such as Mercedes and Benz had to make a completely new start. The war had one benefit for Mercedes, however: it learned a lot about supercharging as a means of improving the power of aero engines without adding much weight. The Daimler company had begun intensive work on supercharging in 1915 and by the end of the war knew as much as anybody about this exciting new method of increasing performance.

This meant that the company was able to introduce two rapid new road cars in 1921: the 6/25/40 and the 10/40/65, of 1568 cc and 2614 cc respectively. The nomenclature was quite logical once you knew how the Mercedes supercharging system worked. The first number represented the German fiscal horsepower figure; the second the peak power with the supercharger disengaged; and the third the maximum with the supercharger in operation.

Both models used a Roots twin-blade supercharger which was, in effect, two closely meshing figure-of-eight vanes that forced air into the engine's induction system under pressure. When mixed with fuel in the right quantity, more power was produced because more of the mixture could be forced in than when under only atmospheric pressure. The loading on the engine, particularly the cylinder head, was increased, but the Mercedes units were so strongly made that they could resist such extra pressure. This was not the case with the products of some of its competitors!

The Roots air pump, or supercharger, was mounted vertically at the front of the engine and driven at about three times the speed of the crankshaft. It was engaged through a small clutch by a mechanical linkage once the accelerator pedal had been floored. Superchargers tended to be very noisy in operation, making a distinctive scream. Thus, when a supercharged Mercedes overtook a slower car, it frequently did so with an ear-splitting howl as the supercharger was engaged for a brief burst of extra power!

Both new cars used four-cylinder engines and relatively conventional chassis. Although they were fast for their day, the performance was not exceptional when viewed with hindsight because they invariably carried very solid and heavy coachwork. The car illustrated is one of the lightest models available; it weighs in at more than 2035 kg (2 tons)!

ENGINE		CHASSIS	
Type	In-line, water-cooled	Frame	Channel section, cross-braced
No. of cylinders	4		
Bore/stroke mm	80 × 130	Wheelbase mm	3050
Displacement cc	2614	Track – front mm	1340
Valve operation	2 per cylinder, overhead camshaft	Track – rear mm	1300
		Suspension – front	Half-elliptic springs, beam axle
Sparkplugs per cyl.	1		
Compression ratio	5:1	Suspension – rear	Half-elliptic springs, live axle
Induction	Mercedes carburettor, Roots supercharger	Brakes	Drums front and rear
		PERFORMANCE	
BHP	65	Maximum speed	110 km/h (68.4 mph)
Transmission	Four-speed manual gearbox	Fuel consumption	24 litres/100 km (11.8 mpg)

1926 Mercedes-Benz 24/100/140K

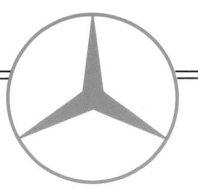

Mercedes-Benz 24/100/140K

Following the merger of the Daimler and Benz concern, development continued on the supercharged Mercedes cars as top-line models of the new Mercedes-Benz range. Profit margins were high on each car built, but production was restricted because so much work went into their beautiful construction – and there were few people who could afford them in any case. So the supercharged Mercedes-Benz continued in ever more exotic form, produced in tiny numbers.

One of the main problems with the 24/100/140 was that its handling could be alarming in the extreme under provocation. As a result, reduction in weight became a greater priority than extracting more power from its already formidable engine. One of the first changes was to shorten the chassis for the new 24/100/140 model in 1926, called K for *kurz* (short). This reduced the weight of the rolling chassis to a mere 1525 kg (1½ tons), or 2035 kg (2 tons) with a touring body. The overtaxed brakes, which had had to deal with 2300 kg (2¼ tons) on the longer-wheelbase car, thus became marginally better and were made a good deal more efficient by detail development, which included eliminating a separate set of shoes for the handbrake.

Subsequent evolution of this theme included the 24/110/160K in 1928, which had a more powerful version of the 6.24-litre engine, and was still aimed chiefly at customers in the affluent high-speed touring market.

During the previous two years another line of development had been followed for customers who wanted an outright sports car and did not mind almost stepping down into it. This was the 26/120/180S introduced in 1926 with the shorter wheelbase, a far lower chassis, and a 6.8-litre version of the existing six-cylinder engine. Although it was of basically the same construction, this much lighter S-for-Sport model weighed in at only 1900 kg (1¾ tons), had a less luxurious body and felt like a completely different car. It even managed to look different when fitted with the same touring or cabriolet bodywork as the 26/100/140K or 26/110/160K, simply because it was so much lower.

The reason for this was that the chassis of the S had been redesigned to sweep up high over the rear axle, allowing the side rails on which everything else was mounted to run much lower. The resultant lowering of the centre of gravity, especially with the sports bodywork, transformed the handling.

ENGINE		CHASSIS	
Type	In-line, water-cooled	**Frame**	Channel section, cross-braced
No. of cylinders	6		
Bore/stroke mm	94 × 150	**Wheelbase mm**	3400
Displacement cc	6240	**Track – front mm**	1430
Valve operation	2 per cylinder, overhead camshaft	**Track – rear mm**	1430
		Suspension – front	Half-elliptic springs, beam axle
Sparkplugs per cyl.	1		
Compression ratio	5:1	**Suspension – rear**	Half-elliptic springs, live axle
Induction	Mercedes carburettor, Roots supercharger	**Brakes**	Drums front and rear
BHP	140	**PERFORMANCE**	
Transmission	Four-speed manual gearbox	**Maximum speed**	145 km/h (90 mph)
		Fuel consumption	25 litres/100 km (11.3 mpg)

1928 Mercedes-Benz SSK

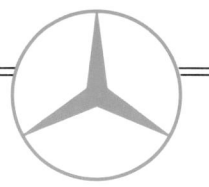

Mercedes-Benz SSK

The engine of the 26/120/180S was bored out in 1928 to give 7065 cc and more power for the 27/140/200 Typ SS: so called because it was Mercedes' Super Sports car. At the same time the cylinder head was redesigned to operate with dual ignition, and later that year with a higher, 6.2:1, compression ratio for even more power as the 27/170/225SS.

Further development included shortening the still long chassis to a 2950 mm (9 ft 8 in) wheelbase for a car which became the legendary SSK with the option of either engine: the lower-powered for touring, the higher for racing. It was an SSK (Super Sports Short) in which aces such as Rudolf Caracciola sprang to prominence despite the still woefully inadequate brakes. Caracciola's brilliant driving was never better illustrated than during the 1928 German Grand Prix when he won on the notoriously tricky Nürburgring with an SS, or in taking third place on the tortuous road circuit of the Monaco Grand Prix in 1930 with an SSK against the far more agile Bugattis. In the same year he demolished the previously all-conquering blower Bentleys during Britain's oldest road race, the Tourist Trophy in Ulster, and then produced an epic solo win in the 1931 Mille Miglia over about 1600 km – 1000 (old Roman) miles – of rough Italian roads and mountain passes.

By this time the SSK had been further developed as the even rarer SSKL (Super Sports Short Light), with power increased at the expense of reliability, through the 27/180/250SSK of 1929, to the ultimate 27/240/300SSKL of 1930, which had an even higher, 7:1, compression ratio. The higher the ratio was raised the bigger the blast inside the cylinder and the more power became available – until the top was literally blown off the engine. This made the maximum power output usable for only short bursts and meant that the engine had to be rebuilt or replaced after every race. In this form, the weight having been pared down through 1700 kg (1⅔ tons) for the SSK to only 1500 kg (1½ tons) for the SSKL, maximum speeds of 235 km/h (146 mph) – and even higher with fully streamlined bodywork – were seen on banked tracks like that at the AVUS, where handling and visibility were of less importance than outright speed.

In the light of these thoroughbred offspring, the SSK with its 6.2:1 compression ratio engine and the lightweight sports bodywork can be seen as an absolute classic, one of the greatest road racing cars ever built.

ENGINE		CHASSIS	
Type	In-line, water-cooled	**Frame**	Channel section, box-braced
No. of cylinders	6		
Bore/stroke mm	100 × 150	**Wheelbase mm**	2950
Displacement cc	7069	**Track – front mm**	1418
Valve operation	2 per cylinder, overhead camshaft	**Track – rear mm**	1418
		Suspension – front	Half-elliptic springs, beam axle
Sparkplugs per cyl.	2		
Compression ratio	6.2:1	**Suspension – rear**	Half-elliptic springs, live axle
Induction	2 Pallas carburettors, Roots supercharger	**Brakes**	Drums front and rear
BHP	225		
Transmission	Four-speed manual gearbox	**PERFORMANCE**	
		Maximum speed	201 km/h (125 mph)
		Fuel consumption	23.5 litres/100 km (12 mpg)

1931 Mercedes-Benz Mannheim 370S

Mercedes-Benz Mannheim 370S

Once Mercedes and Benz were well on the way to merger they began to rationalize their ranges. At the same time, the Benz body-building works closed and production was transferred to the under-used, but more modern, Mercedes body plant at Sindelfingen, near Stuttgart.

Planning for new models to be produced at the main Benz works in Mannheim and the Mercedes plant at Stuttgart continued at the same time. These new models, which were launched in October 1926 (only three months after the formal merger had been completed) were more like the solid middle-of-the-road Benz antecedents than most of the more exciting Mercedes. They both had six-cylinder engines, of 2-litre and 3.1-litre displacement; the smaller – and shorter – car was called the Stuttgart, after the factory where it was built, and the larger the Mannheim, after its home plant. Both used conventional chassis with a full range of open and closed bodywork, carrying flat radiators like the former Benz, but of similar outline to the Mercedes. It was as effective a way of combining the two companies' trademarks as the three-pointed star in a laurel wreath circle above the radiator.

The Mannheim was an altogether more expensive model than the cheaper Stuttgart and used more alloy in its engine, as well as being fitted with a four-speed, rather than a three-speed, gearbox. Subsequently, the engines of these two cars were enlarged in stages to 2.6 litres and 3.5 litres by 1928 to become the Stuttgart 260 and the Mannheim 350. Then the Mannheim's power unit was increased yet again to 3.7 litres for the 370 in 1930. This model was made available initially with saloon or open touring bodywork as the 370, or with more sporting coachwork on the model known as the 370K; a genuinely short-wheelbase variant, the 370S, was introduced later in 1930. It was amusing to note that this car used the Stuttgart chassis!

Although it bore the same 15/75 nomenclature as the other Mannheims, and was never officially given the K designation because a Stuttgart already had it, the 370S possessed a more sporting character due to its lighter weight, nimbler handling and twin-carburettor engine. In fact, it went a long way towards bridging the gap between the Benz-style Stuttgart and Mannheim ranges and the Mercedes-type top cars. The Mannheim 370S was generally fitted with more attractive bodywork than the other 370s, in either the roadster or the sports-cabriolet form shown.

ENGINE		CHASSIS	
Type	In-line, water-cooled	**Frame**	Channel section, cross-braced
No. of cylinders	6		
Bore/stroke mm	82.5 × 115	**Wheelbase mm**	3689
Displacement cc	3689	**Track – front mm**	1425
Valve operation	2 per cylinder, side, pushrod	**Track – rear mm**	1425
		Suspension – front	Half-elliptic springs, beam axle
Sparkplugs per cyl.	1		
Compression ratio	5.5:1	**Suspension – rear**	Half-elliptic springs, live axle
Induction	2 *Flachstromvergaser* carburettors		
		Brakes	Drums front and rear
BHP	75		
Transmission	Four-speed manual gearbox	PERFORMANCE	
		Maximum speed	115 km/h (71.4 mph)
		Fuel consumption	18.5 litres/100 km (15.25 mpg)

1932 Grosser Mercedes

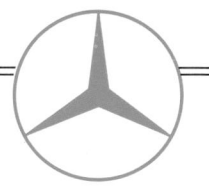

Grosser Mercedes

Former Benz engineering chief Hans Nibel took over from Dr Ferdinand Porsche when he left following a row with senior management. Nibel's first Mercedes-Benz was a truly monumental machine that will never be forgotten: the Typ 770 Grosser Mercedes. This colossus really lived up to its grand name with a weight of more than 3500 kg (3½ tons) and an overall length of around 5200 mm (17 ft). It was powered by an old-style straight-8 engine of 7655 cc that might have seemed more at home in a ship than a car. Its maximum power was delivered at only 2800 rpm and was boosted from 150 to 200 bhp by Mercedes' normal supercharger. A conventional three-speed transmission was linked to a two-speed transfer box, truck style, to give six forward ratios, and the assembly was supplied by Maybach, who made the Grosser Mercedes' only rival, called the Zeppelin after the company's airship work! The Mercedes chassis also took its inspiration from truck practice with an enormous 3940 mm (12 ft 11 in) wheelbase and sturdy half-elliptic cart springs.

The chauffeurs who drove these vehicles had to be very strong to manhandle the steering; they received some assistance, however, in stopping the monsters, from a vacuum servo of the type normally found on a truck, or the Typ 460 Nürburg which had been the Grosser Mercedes' forerunner from 1928. The 460 and larger 500 version continued in production along similar lines to the 770 until 1933.

Only about 100 of the Typ 770 mammoths were built between 1930 and 1937 – as a demonstration of what Mercedes could achieve in a period that had started in deep economic depression. They were not for sale to ordinary people – even if they could have afforded the price of around RM40,000 (without optional armour plating). These cars were reserved for heads of state and celebrities of whom Daimler-Benz approved, including the exiled Kaiser Wilhelm II, first owner of the 1932 Grosser Mercedes shown.

Naturally, Adolf Hitler and high-ranking members of the Nazi party used Grosser Mercedes with open, closed and limousine bodywork. This has led to latter-day claims that almost any Typ 770 that turns up is an ex-*Führerwagen*! It is rather more likely to be one of the cars of the Emperor Hirohito of Japan, who had several and used them well into the 1960s. Later versions of the Grosser Mercedes, built from 1937, had a more advanced tubular chassis and independent suspension.

ENGINE		CHASSIS	
Type	In-line, water-cooled	**Frame**	Box section, cross-braced
No. of cylinders	8		
Bore/stroke mm	96 × 135	**Wheelbase mm**	3940
Displacement cc	7655	**Track – front mm**	1626
Valve operation	2 per cylinder, overhead, pushrod	**Track – rear mm**	1680
		Suspension – front	Independent, wishbone and coil
Sparkplugs per cyl.	1		
Compression ratio	5 : 1	**Suspension – rear**	de Dion, coil
Induction	Mercedes carburettor, Roots supercharger	**Brakes**	Drums front and rear
		PERFORMANCE	
BHP	200	**Maximum speed**	138 km/h (86 mph)
Transmission	Five-speed manual gearbox	**Fuel consumption**	47 litres/100 km (6 mpg)

1934 Mercedes-Benz 500K

Mercedes Benz 500K

As the nimble Bugattis and Alfa Romeos took over in sports car racing, and Mercedes began to build special cars for grand prix events, the prestigious SS and SSK cars evolved into an exotic line of new machines that were intended purely for touring in the grandest manner.

The first of these, the 380S of 1932, was Nibel's last great work before he died the following year. In many ways, it was nearer to being a replacement for the Mannheim 370S, although it superseded the Nürburg 500 at the same time and took much of its technology from the Grosser Mercedes. The 380's 3.8-litre engine, for instance, amounted to a smaller version of the Typ 770's unit.

The chassis was of similar construction, but far lower slung, like the 370S. The suspension, however, was entirely new, and was notable for employing wishbones and coil springs at the front for the first time in a production car. This form of independent front suspension has, of course, gone on to become the most popular in the world. Independent rear suspension was adopted at the same time to give a much more civilized ride, by means of swing axles and coil springs, which were popular then with top Mercedes management. In spite of the geometrical problems inherent in such a system, the resultant handling was far superior to that of either the SSK or the Grosser Mercedes.

Despite its smaller engine, and pretensions, the 380S was still an incredibly heavy car; its chassis alone weighed around 1575 kg (1½ tons), with very luxurious bodywork as standard adding another 1000 kg (1 ton) or more.

This bodywork, usually built at Sindelfingen, took the form of either an extravagantly styled coupé, a magnificent open tourer, a conventionally dignified coupé, a soft-top cabriolet or one of the most luxurious saloons you could imagine.

Around 120 km/h (75 mph) was the best speed that could be extracted from such a substantial car: this was in fact very good for its day. But it was not good enough for those people who had savoured the thrills of the earlier sporting Mercedes, and the 380S was supercharged in the same way the following year. In this form, it was known as the 380K (for *Kompressor*, this time, not *kurz*) with the power raised to 120 bhp from 80 bhp. A larger capacity (4019 cc) engine was also listed at the same time in 1933 to give more torque, before the standard displacement was raised to 5019 cc for the 500K in 1934.

ENGINE		CHASSIS	
Type	In-line, water-cooled	**Frame**	Box section, cross-braced
No. of cylinders	8		
Bore/stroke mm	86 × 108	**Wheelbase mm**	3290
Displacement cc	5019	**Track – front mm**	1510
Valve operation	2 per cylinder, overhead, pushrod	**Track – rear mm**	1500
		Suspension – front	Independent, wishbone and coil
Sparkplugs per cyl.	1		
Compression ratio	5:1	**Suspension – rear**	Independent, swing axle and coil
Induction	Mercedes carburettor, Roots supercharger	**Brakes**	Drums front and rear
BHP	160	**PERFORMANCE**	
Transmission	Four-speed manual gearbox	**Maximum speed**	161 km/h (100 mph)
		Fuel consumption	35.3 litres/100 km (8 mpg)

1936 Mercedes-Benz 540K

Mercedes-Benz 540K

Work on the 500K's successor went on for two years as differing forms of suspension were tried. One of the prototypes used between 1934 and 1936 had a racing car-style de Dion system at the back which eliminated the undesirable camber changes associated with swing axles. It was made ready for production, then killed at the last moment by senior management, which decreed that swing axles should be retained in line with other Mercedes products. A still larger version of the straight-8 engine was retained, however, to take the maximum speed up to 171 km/h (106 mph), an almost unheard-of performance for a road car in those days. On introduction in 1936, the Mercedes 540K became the fastest standard production car in the world.

Its steering was very heavy at low speeds, but became lighter and much more manageable above 64 km/h (40 mph). It was almost impossible to change gear when the oil was cold, but once it had warmed up you could change between the two top ratios without using the clutch, so sweet was the action.

Many variants on the 540K theme were made until the enforced cessation of production in 1942. A lightweight version clocked 180 km/h (112 mph) in 1937, although most 540Ks carried similar heavyweight bodies to those used on the 500K. Long- and short wheelbase versions were made: the longer footing was retained for saloons, the shorter – standard from 1938 – for coupés. An engine with its displacement enlarged to 5800 cc was built in 1939, and a very short series of 600Ks made between 1938 and 1942. They had the same variety of bodywork, but were fitted with V12-cylinder engines of 6020 cc that produced a maximum of 240 bhp when their superchargers were engaged. There was little difference in performance, but they were even smoother than the straight-8s. They also had a five-speed all-synchromesh gearbox, seen on later Typ 770 Grosser Mercedes versions from 1937.

These Typ 770 cars bore a close resemblance to the very rare 600K V12, the chief difference outwardly being that they were slightly bigger. It is interesting to note that the later 770s used the rear suspension that had been developed for the prototype 540K, allied to a new tubular frame which would have transformed the coupé into a much lighter and more agile machine. Only one 580K-engined 540K has been seen at auction since World War 2, so it is hardly surprising that examples of the normal 540Ks have set record prices at auctions in recent years.

ENGINE		CHASSIS	
Type	In-line, water-cooled	**Frame**	Box section, cross-braced
No. of cylinders	8		
Bore/stroke mm	88 × 111	**Wheelbase mm**	3290
Displacement cc	5401	**Track – front mm**	1510
Valve operation	2 per cylinder, overhead, pushrod	**Track – rear mm**	1500
		Suspension – front	Independent, wishbone and coil
Sparkplugs per cyl.	1		
Compression ratio	5 : 1	**Suspension – rear**	Independent, swing axle and coil
Induction	Mercedes carburettor, Roots supercharger	**Brakes**	Drums front and rear
BHP	180	**PERFORMANCE**	
Transmission	Four-speed manual gearbox	**Maximum speed**	171 km/h (106 mph)
		Fuel consumption	35.3 litres/100 km (8 mpg)

1938 Mercedes-Benz 230

Mercedes-Benz 230

The glamorous supercharged Mercedes represented only a tiny proportion of the company's production, most of it being made up by cars such as the Typ 170 introduced in 1931. Although it had a six-cylinder engine and some very advanced features, the 170's styling was unimaginative to say the least. It had a normal box-section chassis but, amazingly, independent suspension on all four wheels! This was achieved by the use of a transverse leaf spring at the front and by swing axles at the back. Modern easy-to-clean, and cheaper-to-make, solid steel disc wheels were fitted in place of the spoked type normally found on cars at the time. The side-valve engine produced only 32 bhp, limiting maximum speed to 88 km/h (55 mph), but the Typ 170's behaviour on the road was far more refined than most cars in that era. The geometrical problems caused by the swing axles' wide range of movement were of little significance in a car of such modest performance.

Other notable technical achievements on the Typ 170 included the use of hydraulic brakes and central chassis lubrication.

Two years later, pleas for more power were answered by the introduction of the Typ 200 with a 2-litre version of the engine. This faster model immediately sold better than the 170 and was uprated again to 2229 cc to give the 230 a top speed of 121 km/h (75 mph) in 1936.

Further technological advances included using the 230 as the basis for the world's first mass-produced diesel car. In this case the normal six-cylinder engine was replaced by a 2.6-litre four-cylinder compression-ignition unit that was far more civilized in operation than earlier versions.

Running on a 20.5 : 1 compression ratio with Bosch fuel injection, this engine produced only 45 bhp against the 55 of the 2.3-litre petrol unit, but used less fuel. As a result, the 260D, as the diesel car was known, became an immediate favourite with high-mileage users, particularly taxicab operators, and established Mercedes-Benz with a lead in this field it has never relinquished.

At about the same time, a new tubular chassis was designed for the 230 with a backbone formation to work better in conjunction with the established suspension. Despite difficulties with rear suspension, these cars can be seen to be among the most advanced in the world before World War 2.

ENGINE		CHASSIS	
Type	In-line, water-cooled	Frame	Tubular backbone
No. of cylinders	6	Wheelbase mm	2540
Bore/stroke mm	72.5 × 90	Track – front mm	1340
Displacement cc	2229	Track – rear mm	1340
Valve operation	Side	Suspension – front	Independent, transverse leaf spring
Sparkplugs per cyl.	1		
Compression ratio	7 : 1	Suspension – rear	Independent, swing axle and coil
Induction	Mercedes carburettor		
BHP	55	Brakes	Drums front and rear
Transmission	Four-speed manual gearbox		
		PERFORMANCE	
		Maximum speed	121 km/h (75 mph)
		Fuel consumption	12.28 litres/100 km (23 mpg)

1939 Mercedes-Benz W163

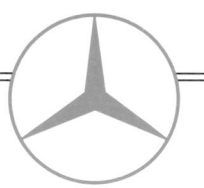

Mercedes-Benz W163

Daimler-Benz had substantial government support when it re-entered grand prix racing with a purpose-built car for a new formula that stipulated a 750 kg (1653 lb) maximum weight limit. But the subsidy hardly covered the cost of the exotic cars that followed. Mercedes managed to liberate a lot more power than expected from engines built from very light alloys to keep down their weight. The result was a series of incredibly fast cars with maximum speeds approaching 320 km/h (200 mph) under pressure of rivalry from the German Auto Unions designed by Dr Ferdinand Porsche.

The first of these Mercedes grand prix cars, designed by Hans Nibel, was the W25 with a rigid lightweight frame, wishbone-and-coil and swing-axle independent suspension all round, and combined gearbox and rear axle – or transaxle – to balance the weight of its 3.3-litre supercharged straight-8 engine. It developed 314 bhp in its earliest form to share a number of grand prix wins with Auto Union, the rival Alfa Romeos and Bugattis being eclipsed. Ever-larger engines took the power to 430 bhp for 1935 and a highly streamlined example driven by Caracciola broke the world flying kilometre record at 317.60 km/h (197.35 mph).

The Mercedes team led by Caracciola won practically everything in 1935 before facing a far more serious threat from Auto Union with new V16-cylinder cars in 1936. As a result, the W25 was redesigned for 1937 as the W125 (which had originally been intended as a smaller 3-litre car) with an amazing 600 bhp 5.6-litre straight-8 engine. Swing-axle suspension could not cope with such power, so the de Dion layout that appeared on the Grosser Mercedes was adopted to eliminate the loss of adhesion that resulted from dramatic camber changes. These cars also had a limited-slip differential of a type that was to become mandatory on really high performance cars.

A 3-litre supercharged limit was imposed for 1938, but the awe-inspiring Mercedes grand prix cars lost little of their speed, thanks to a new V12-cylinder engine and improvements to their handling, braking and streamlining. Eventually the W154, as the new model was called, was honed to its finest degree as the W163 grand prix car of 1939. This 483 bhp machine won five of its seven big races that year. It remains the ultimate racing car, in every sense, built before World War 2.

ENGINE		CHASSIS	
Type	V, water-cooled	**Frame**	Tubular construction
No. of cylinders	12	**Wheelbase mm**	2540
Bore/stroke mm	67 × 70	**Track – front mm**	1575
Displacement cc	2962	**Track – rear mm**	1524
Valve operation	4 per cylinder, twin overhead camshafts	**Suspension – front**	Independent, wishbone and coil
Sparkplugs per cyl.	1	**Suspension – rear**	de Dion, torsion bar
Compression ratio	5.75 : 1	**Brakes**	Drums front and rear
Induction	Mercedes triple-choke carburettor, 2 Roots superchargers		
		PERFORMANCE	
BHP	483	**Maximum speed**	315.5 km/h (196 mph)
Transmission	Five-speed manual gearbox	**Fuel consumption**	94.16 litres/100 km (3 mpg)

1954 Mercedes-Benz 220

Mercedes-Benz 220

Daimler-Benz factories were badly damaged by Allied bombing raids during World War 2 and it was not until 1948 that car production went back into full swing with the pre-war 170V as mainstay. This was extensively redesigned in 1949 as the 170S, with a modified chassis retaining the cruciform layout of oval-section tubes linked to outriggers to carry saloon or cabriolet bodywork. The opportunity was taken to deal with three main problems that had arisen when the car was extended to its limits: violent camber change in the rear suspension, which could lead to one wheel tucking under with a dramatic loss of adhesion; axle tramp at the front resulting in a speed wobble; and a general lack of power from what was becoming a very dated engine.

The necessity to increase the engine's power – by 37 per cent to 52 bhp – also heightened the difficulties with the suspension. This was improved by increasing the rear track by 127 mm (5 in) and replacing the transverse leaf spring arrangement at the front with wishbone and coil springs like those used on the 540K and grand prix cars. The 170S that resulted was still not a fast car, but it felt a lot more stable when cruising along an *Autobahn* than the 170V!

Detail modifications to the engine and high overall gearing also enabled the 170S to be driven flat out almost indefinitely on Germany's growing network of new motorways, which mitigated the relatively modest maximum speed of 120 km/h (75 mph). A 1700 cc diesel version also became very popular and helped Mercedes re-establish itself as a manufacturer of high-quality cars.

As the hardships brought about by the war were reduced in what was now West Germany through hard work, so people became more affluent, and the 170S was uprated. The 220 introduced in 1951 with the larger 300 and 300S carried on the improvements initiated on the earlier car. The chassis was strengthened and given a still wider track, and a new 2.2-litre six-cylinder engine was adopted to give 80 bhp. This was a much more modern unit than the old side-valve engine, with a more efficient chain-driven overhead camshaft and a short stroke to enable it to rev faster. The new engine lost some of the 'chugging' ability of the older unit, but this was of little importance to the majority of customers who now spent more of their lives on motorways than on the often appalling tracks that had been called roads but a few years earlier.

ENGINE		CHASSIS	
Type	In-line, water-cooled	**Frame**	Tubular backbone
No. of cylinders	6	**Wheelbase mm**	2750
Bore/stroke mm	80 × 72.33	**Track – front mm**	1470
Displacement cc	2195	**Track – rear mm**	1485
Valve operation	2 per cylinder, single overhead camshaft	**Suspension – front**	Independent, wishbone and coil
Sparkplugs per cyl.	1	**Suspension – rear**	Independent, swing axle and coil
Compression ratio	6.5 : 1		
Induction	Stromberg carburettor	**Brakes**	Drums front and rear
		PERFORMANCE	
BHP	80	**Maximum speed**	129 km/h (80 mph)
Transmission	Four-speed manual gearbox	**Fuel consumption**	11.5 litres/100 km (25 mpg)

1955 Mercedes-Benz 300SL

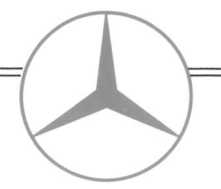

Mercedes-Benz 300SL

Mercedes saw a competition programme as part of the postwar process of re-establishing its reputation for producing some of the world's fastest cars. The 220 would have had to be modified beyond all recognition to achieve much success in sports car racing, which offered the best opportunities for publicity at the time. Touring car races for saloons were in their infancy and long-distance rallies were still severely hampered by the scarcities of fuel and tyres prevailing at the time. So the six-cylinder engine of the 300S was taken as the major component for a new sports car, an especially attractive move when it was found that it could be made to run well when canted over to one side. This gave a low bonnet line, making possible wind-cheating bodywork which would compensate for the lack of horsepower against pure racing units. There was also a virtue in being able to point out that largely standard components were used in a successful competition car. For the same reason, suspension similar to that of the production cars was retained, including their flexible kingpost mountings, which allowed slight fore and aft cushioning of the wishbones. The swing axle's geometry was also changed to lower the roll centre and make the new car more stable. It was not intended to produce many of these cars, so a spaceframe chassis of thin steel tubing was used even though it took many hours of skilled labour to build. The ultra-lightweight aluminium gullwing-doored coupé body was an even greater work of art and fully justified the new car's title of 300SL (for 3-litre *Sport Leicht*).

With such ordinary basic components, it was not the fastest sports car of its day, but it was so strong and reliable that it won four of the five major events it contested in 1952. Along with the smaller Porsches, Mercedes could claim to have the most dependable cars in competition – which did its reputation no harm!

A vast amount of engineering time was needed to enter higher realms, however, where lightly modified production components were inadequate. This prompted the factory to withdraw from racing for a while to concentrate on building new racing cars. But it would have been a pity not to capitalize on the 300SL's success, so the company introduced a limited production version that retained many of the competition car's features but had the advantage of 40 bhp more from the latest Bosch fuel injection.

ENGINE		CHASSIS	
Type	In-line, canted block, water-cooled	**Frame**	Tubular spaceframe
No. of cylinders	6	**Wheelbase mm**	2400
Bore/stroke mm	85 × 88	**Track – front mm**	1398
Displacement cc	2996	**Track – rear mm**	1448
Valve operation	2 per cylinder, overhead camshaft	**Suspension – front**	Independent, wishbone and coil
Sparkplugs per cyl.	1	**Suspension – rear**	Independent, swing axle and coil
Compression ratio	8.55 : 1	**Brakes**	Drums front and rear
Induction	Bosch fuel injection		
BHP	215	**PERFORMANCE**	
Transmission	Four-speed manual gearbox	**Maximum speed**	265 km/h (165 mph)
		Fuel consumption	19 litres/100 km (15 mpg)

1955 Mercedes-Benz 300SLR

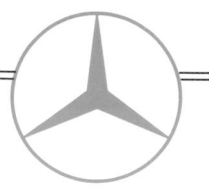

Mercedes-Benz 300SLR

Daimler-Benz, suitably encouraged by the success of the 300SL, committed itself to an expensive top-line racing programme with the advent of a new 2½-litre Formula 1 in 1954. To keep the weight of the heaviest component – the engine – to a minimum, the company again opted for a straight-8, lying almost on its side, and thus allowing a low bonnet line. Although this unit followed traditional Mercedes practice, it was unusual in that it had desmodromic valve gear in which the valves were opened and closed by a clever system of cams and rockers, eliminating the normal valve springs which were prone to give trouble.

The new W196 grand prix car used a spaceframe like the 300SL with, surprisingly, swing-axle rear suspension as on the production cars to demonstrate that it was possible to make this layout work well in a high-performance machine. Drum brakes were retained (although the rival British Jaguars were achieving wonders with discs) because Mercedes could make the drums itself.

The W196 enjoyed a great deal of success with the option of dramatic all-enveloping or stumpy open-wheeled bodywork, depending on the nature of individual circuits. High-speed circuits saw the W196 in streamlined form, and tighter circuits the lighter, less bulky bodywork. Former world champion Juan Manuel Fangio

brought out the best in these cars to take the title for a second time and the manufacturers' award for Mercedes.

Daimler-Benz was encouraged to continue with the W196 for 1955 with the addition of a new 300SLR sports car for the top long-distance races, such as Le Mans. Although the 300SLR was very similar in concept to the W196, it was quite different in detail. Its straight-8 desmodromic engine had a totally different form of cylinder block with the capacity raised to 2976 cc, to give far more torque. The spaceframe followed the W196's lines, except that the wheelbase was adjustable for fast or tight circuits, and the brakes were augmented by a hydraulically raised flap at the back. This worked well on fast circuits.

The W196 continued on its winning ways in 1955 as the 300SLR became equally famous, taking the Mille Miglia for the British driver Stirling Moss. The 300SLRs, though, were withdrawn at Le Mans that year following the worst accident in the history of motor racing, when over 80 people were killed as Pierre Levegh's 300SLR crashed into the crowd. They won other events in 1955, however, and went on to take their world title as did the W196, at which point Daimler-Benz retired from competition well satisfied with its demonstration of technical excellence.

ENGINE		CHASSIS	
Type	In-line, water-cooled	Frame	Tubular spaceframe
No. of cylinders	8	Wheelbase mm	2476
Bore/stroke mm	78 × 78	Track – front mm	1448
Displacement cc	2982	Track – rear mm	1448
Valve operation	2 per cylinder, desmodromic operation	Suspension – front	Independent, wishbone and torsion bar
Sparkplugs per cyl.	2	Suspension – rear	Independent, swing axle and coil
Compression ratio	12 : 1		
Induction	Bosch fuel injection	Brakes	Inboard drums front and rear
BHP	296		
Transmission	Five-speed transaxle		

PERFORMANCE	
Maximum speed	290 km/h (180 mph)
Fuel consumption	56.5 litres/100 km (5 mpg)

1964 Mercedes-Benz 220SE coupé

Mercedes-Benz 220SE coupé

Once Mercedes had shown a brave new world what brilliant racing cars it could make, the company set about revitalizing its normal products. The general policy was not to introduce an entirely new car, but to update existing ones with fresh running gear, and then to phase in new bodies and styles. In this way, the 170 became the 180 in 1953, featuring Mercedes' first full-width bodyshell. This was of modern integral construction in which the geometrical elements of the previous tubular frame were incorporated in the basic structure. These shells had to be made from a variety of pressed-steel parts, which were then welded together. The giant presses to stamp out such parts and the jigs in which the bodies were built cost a great deal of money, and the investment could only be recouped when such bodies were produced in large quantities. The old type of tubular frame cost less to make in small numbers, and continued to feature in principle on the racing cars and exclusively top-line models. But there came a point when the cost of the labour needed to make the tubular frames overtook the cost of the investment in a unitary bodyshell. The balance was then tipped in favour of the more modern design because it was also stronger and allowed the use of softer suspension, and this promoted better handling.

Once the major hurdle of launching the new form of construction had been cleared, the 180 became the 190 with the more modern overhead-camshaft engine – and a slightly more powerful 220 version was introduced. This appealed to middle-class people buying a car part way between the cheaper 190 and the expensive 300. Numerous variants were made on each theme: for example a standard 220 with 105 bhp, a Super version (220S) with 124 bhp, and a 220SE (for *Super Einspritz*, or Super with fuel injection) sporting 130 bhp.

The established swing-axle rear suspension was refined still further for safer handling. Subsequently these production saloons and tourers – restyled with distinctive rear fins in 1959 – were augmented by a coupé and convertible with two-door bodywork in 1961. The frontal aspect remained the same with dominant vertically stacked lighting, but the rear wings were considered far more elegant with rounded tops. In this form, the 220SE coupé became one of the most desirable Mercedes four-seaters of its era.

ENGINE		CHASSIS	
Type	In-line, water-cooled	Frame	Unitary construction
No. of cylinders	6	Wheelbase mm	2750
Bore/stroke mm	80 × 72.8	Track – front mm	1482
Displacement cc	2197	Track – rear mm	1485
Valve operation	2 per cylinder, single overhead camshaft	Suspension – front	Independent, wishbone and coil
Sparkplugs per cyl.	1	Suspension – rear	Independent, swing axle and coil
Compression ratio	8.7:1		
Induction	Bosch fuel injection	Brakes	Discs front, drums rear
BHP	120		
Transmission	Four-speed manual or automatic gearbox		
		PERFORMANCE	
		Maximum speed	170 km/h (105.6 mph)
		Fuel consumption	10.7 litres/100 km (26.4 mpg)

1965 Mercedes-Benz 230SL

Mercedes-Benz 230SL

Contrary to popular belief, the Mercedes-Benz 230SL was a completely new car, owing little to the earlier 190SL which directly preceded it, or to the 300SL which ceased production on its introduction in 1963. The 190SL was simply a sporting version of the 190 saloon and rather slow and ponderous as a result, whereas the 300SL in its early 1960s roadster form was a development of the spaceframe gullwing cars which had been outlawed by fears that their occupants might be trapped if the car overturned and landed on its roof.

The 230SL was essentially a Grand Touring car based on the 220SE saloon. Daimler-Benz saw it as a sophisticated machine for two people sharing expensive tastes who wanted a car to convey them with their luggage over long distances at reasonably high speeds: the last thing such customers would want was a wind-in-the-neck, shaking, smoking sports car. The 230SL had all the comforts of one of Mercedes top saloons, such as power-assisted steering and the option of automatic transmission. It was more than anything a GT car, with the appearance of a light, lithe sports car. It was far from being a ponderous saloon!

It still had swing-axle rear suspension, but at last Mercedes was able to demonstrate that it had tamed all the vagaries of this arrangement with cleverly reset geometry. It also had what seemed to be enormous tyres (185-14) for its day – which were, of course, part of the taming process. And it had disc brakes (at the front and made by Girling in Britain) for the first time on any Mercedes car.

Despite the excellent engineering, it was the styling that was the best part of the 230SL: it looked astonishingly good, with no hint of the massive lines that had dominated Mercedes production cars for so long. This was achieved on the striking new coupé partly by abandoning the traditional German radiator grille. The 300SL-style flattened air intake that resulted was, however, dominated by an even bigger three-pointed star!

But the element that people remember more than any about the 230SL was the shape of its detachable hard-top: it reminded everybody of a pagoda. When they debated why Mercedes should want to depress the centre of the roof they rarely discovered the true reason: it was a purely functional decision to raise the edges of the roof and make the doors bigger so that the occupants did not have to stoop to enter!

ENGINE		CHASSIS	
Type	In-line, water-cooled	**Frame**	Unitary construction
No. of cylinders	6	**Wheelbase mm**	2400
Bore/stroke mm	82 × 72.8	**Track – front mm**	1474
Displacement cc	2306	**Track – rear mm**	1487
Valve operation	2 per cylinder, single overhead camshaft	**Suspension – front**	Independent, wishbone and coil
Sparkplugs per cyl.	1	**Suspension – rear**	Independent, swing axle and coil
Compression ratio	9.3:1		
Induction	Bosch fuel injection	**Brakes**	Discs front, drums rear
BHP	170		
Transmission	Four-speed manual or automatic gearbox	**PERFORMANCE**	
		Maximum speed	200 km/h (124.3 mph)
		Fuel consumption	15 litres/100 km (18.8 mpg)

1976 Mercedes-Benz 450SEL

Mercedes-Benz 450SEL

Around 50,000 examples of the SL in 230, and later 250 and 280 forms had been sold when the series was replaced in 1971 by a new V8-engined open 350SL and a 350SLC coupé. Both had striking wedge-shaped bodies and new running gear, including semi-trailing arm rear suspension. At last Mercedes had brought its handling up to date!

One of the reasons for sticking to swing axles for so long had been the company's desire to produce something for everybody in the quality motoring world. The amount of engineering time spent developing the range was staggering. Although diesel cars in the 200/220 range made up the bulk of production, there was an incredible number of permutations that could be made on petrol-engined themes.

There were basic carburettor four-cylinder engines, normally aspirated and fuel-injected sixes from 2.3 to 2.8 litres, and injected V8s of 3.5 and 6.3 litres, which could be switched between saloon, coupé or convertible bodyshells with automatic or manual transmission and seemingly endless variations on trim.

In common with all the big manufacturers, ever-tightening American emission laws dominated Mercedes' thinking in the late 1960s and early 1970s. Such a massive market could not be ignored and as a first attempt to satisfy it, two low-emission twin-cam 2.8-litre six-cylinder engines were introduced in 1972. Once these had proved themselves in existing saloons and coupés they were adopted for a new top line of super saloons called the S series. These cars were as near perfection as Mercedes could make them.

They still bore some outward resemblance to a new generation of cheaper models, although they incorporated many detail improvements affecting strength, safety, economy, comfort and refinement. The bodyshell, for instance, incorporated a safety cell to improve the occupants' chances of escaping unscathed from the most violent impacts. And accidents became easier to avoid thanks to a new version of Daimler-Benz's own power steering which set the standards for all others.

Although the 350 models coped quite well with the constrictions of stringent emission laws, Mercedes went one step further in 1973 by introducing a 450 series of 4.5-litre V8s to ensure that no performance was lost. The long-wheelbase 450SEL then became the company's ultimate car.

ENGINE		CHASSIS	
Type	V, water-cooled	**Frame**	Unitary construction
No. of cylinders	8	**Wheelbase mm**	2960
Bore/stroke mm	92 × 85	**Track – front mm**	1520
Displacement cc	4520 cc	**Track – rear mm**	1500
Valve operation	2 per cylinder, single overhead camshaft on each bank	**Suspension – front**	Independent, wishbone and coil
Sparkplugs per cyl.	1	**Suspension – rear**	Independent, semi-trailing arms, coil
Compression ratio	8.8:1	**Brakes**	Discs front and rear
Induction	Bosch fuel injection		
BHP	225	**PERFORMANCE**	
Transmission	Automatic gearbox	**Maximum speed**	210 km/h (130 mph)
		Fuel consumption	14.5 litres/100 km (19.5 mpg)

1980 Mercedes-Benz 450SLC

Mercedes-Benz 450SLC

The popular six-cylinder Mercedes SL grand tourers were replaced in 1971 by new V8-engined cars, the 350SL and a longer-wheelbase fixed-head coupé, the 350SLC. These were soon developed into the 450s, with the larger V8 power unit, the SLC remaining in production until 1980. As the most expensive model in the company's normal range, Mercedes gave it as many individual features as possible. Although it had a longer wheelbase than the SL, to allow more room for the rear-seat passengers, the SLC was still slightly shorter than the basic four-seater SE models.

Mercedes saw its close-coupled fixed-head coupé as a 'personal car' and as such equipped it with numerous gadgets for tycoons who had made it to the top. But in a manner typical of Mercedes, the gadgets were not merely gimmicks: they were all functional and useful. The 450SLC had air conditioning that could cope with extremes of climate from Central Africa to the Arctic Circle and, as a novel touch, the door panels were so shaped that air from this unit demisted the side windows as well as the windscreen. The transmission, naturally, was automatic and the variable-ratio power steering was predictable and almost invariably of neutral

characteristic, neither oversteering nor understeering. The disc braking was also power-assisted, to a sensitive degree, and there was a comprehensive Becker radio and stereo stystem that equalled the finest in the world. The layout of the cockpit was considered close to perfection, as was the position of the easily gripped steering wheel.

The seats were upholstered in the best traditional leather. There was a thoroughly modern vacuum restraint which locked the seat tilting mechanism when the engine was running and the doors were closed; at the same time it allowed the rear-seat passengers to override the facility if they wished. The heated rear window element, which of necessity consumed a lot of power, switched itself off automatically as soon as its work was done, and the central locking system incorporated the fuel filler flap.

With such a comprehensive selection of luxurious fittings, the SLC was aimed squarely at a market dominated by Rolls-Royce at the top end and Jaguar at the bottom. It soon established itself as a car which no self-respecting captain of industry, film star, entrepreneur or television personality could afford to be without.

ENGINE		CHASSIS	
Type	V, water-cooled	**Frame**	Unitary construction
No. of cylinders	8	**Wheelbase mm**	2810
Bore/stroke mm	92 × 85	**Track – front mm**	1450
Displacement cc	4520	**Track – rear mm**	1440
Valve operation	2 per cylinder, single overhead camshaft on each bank	**Suspension – front**	Independent, wishbone and coil
		Suspension – rear	Independent, semi-trailing arms and coil
Sparkplugs per cyl.	1		
Compression ratio	8.8 : 1	**Brakes**	Discs front and rear
Induction	Bosch fuel injection		
BHP	217	**PERFORMANCE**	
Transmission	Automatic gearbox	**Maximum speed**	210 km/h (130 mph)
		Fuel consumption	14.5 litres/100 km (19.5 mpg)

1982 Mercedes-Benz 500SEC

Mercedes-Benz 500SEC

Mercedes continued its quest for perfection in the 1970s with research into how the S class cars could be improved. The first evidence of this was a new all-alloy engine, a petrol V8 of 5 litres' capacity that was lighter and more efficient than the 6.9-litre unit it was meant to replace, along with a 3.8-litre version to take over from the existing 4.5-litre. The new 5-litre engine was given a trial run in the 450SLC – as the 450SLC 5.0 – in 1979 before introduction in the new S class cars later that year. Although the new bodyshell seemed similar to the existing one, it had in fact taken a great deal of reshaping and re-engineering. The shell was narrower, with a strong taper from front to back, and a distinctive shovel nose allied to a wedge-shaped overall profile. The result was a 14 per cent reduction in drag, which improved stability in conjunction with the revised profile. The weight of the body was reduced by 50 kg (110 lb) and that of the engine (the 5-litre in place of the 6.9) by 134 kg (295 lb). This, in conjunction with the aerodynamic improvements and a new four-speed automatic transmission, cut the fuel consumption by 10 per cent without compromising performance. This factor was of particular importance when the tightening of North American 'fleet average' fuel consumption figures was considered (i.e. fuel consumption over the whole range). It was no longer acceptable to import expensive cars that used a lot of fuel – even if the owners could afford it and did not complain – because these figures put the smaller vehicles of the range, which sold in larger quantities, at a disadvantage when the average fuel consumption of all models imported by one manufacturer was calculated. Ultimately it could even lead to exclusion from the vital American market.

The longer wheelbase on the new S class cars – of which the fixed-head 500SEC coupé was the top liner – gave more room for passengers at a small expense to luggage accommodation in the shorter boot. The higher lid of this compartment, imparted by the wedge shape, helped here. New seats, larger doors, regrouped switch gear and more wood trim to highlight the plush appointments were just some of the improvements. There were substantial new mouldings for side protection, and new front and rear bumpers that deformed astonishingly and then eased back to their original shape after impact. And there was even a visor for the interior mirror to shield the eyes of the eastbound driver from the glare of the setting sun.

ENGINE		CHASSIS	
Type	V, water-cooled	Frame	Unitrary construction
No. of cylinders	8	Wheelbase mm	2850
Bore/stroke mm	96.5 × 85	Track – front mm	1540
Displacement cc	4973	Track – rear mm	1520
Valve operation	2 per cylinder, single overhead camshaft on each bank	Suspension – front	Independent, wishbone and coil
Sparkplugs per cyl.	1	Suspension – rear	Independent, semi-trailing arm and coil
Compression ratio	9.2:1	Brakes	Discs front and rear
Induction	Bosch fuel injection		
BHP	231	**PERFORMANCE**	
Transmission	Automatic gearbox	Maximum speed	225 km/h (140 mph)
		Fuel consumption	11.4 litres/100 km (24.8 mpg)